REDWOODS

REDWOODS

PETER MURRAY

THE CHILD'S WORLD®, INC.

Photo Credits
Comstock: 6, 19, 23
Dembinsky Photo Associates/Terry Donnelly: 29
Dembinsky Photo Associates/Greg Gawlowski: 9, 10, 20
Dembinsky Photo Associates/Darrell Gulin: 15, 30
Dembinsky Photo Associates/Adam Jones: 26
Dembinsky Photo Associates/John Mielcarek: 13
Robert and Linda Mitchell: 2
Tony Stone Images/Chris Cheadle: 16
Tony Stone Images/Michael Orton: cover
Tony Stone Images/John Warden: 24

Printed in the United States of America.

Library of Congress Cataloging-in-Publication Data
Murray, Peter, 1952 Sept. 29-
Redwoods/Peter Murray
p.   cm.
Includes index.
Summary: Describes the physical characteristics,
and the ability to survive of redwood trees.
ISBN 1-56766-216-1 (lib. bdg.)
1. Redwood--Juvenile literature.   2. Giant sequoia--
Juvenile literature.

TABLE OF CONTENTS

THE BIRTH OF A REDWOOD!

Two thousand years ago, in the place we now call Northern California, a redwood cone released its seeds. The cone was only about as big as an acorn. It grew high in the branches of a *coast redwood* tree. As the cone opened its scales, dozens of tiny seeds fell out. They fell hundreds of feet down through the branches to land on the forest floor.

A redwood cone lies at the bottom of a redwood tree.

Most of the seeds landed on the leaves and sticks covering the forest floor. Some were eaten by mice and insects. But one tiny seed fell upon a patch of bare soil. That night, it rained. The seed swelled with water and sprouted. It sent a root deep into the earth. The sprout opened its thin, pointy needles. A coast redwood tree was born!

Every year the tree grew taller. In five years it was as tall as a man. By its seventy-fifth birthday, the redwood stood 100 feet tall! And that was just the beginning.

A small redwood grows in the forest.

Out of every million redwood seeds, only one survives to become a tree. But that one redwood can live for a very long time. The seed that sprouted 2,000 years ago is still alive today. The tree is now more than 385 feet high. It has survived fires and storms and earthquakes. It is the tallest living thing on our planet.

Coast redwoods grow in northern California and Oregon. Standing in a redwood grove is like being in a forest of tall, reddish brown columns that rise up forever. It feels as if the trees are holding up the sky.

California redwoods seem to rise up forever.

HOW TALL CAN REDWOODS GROW?

The coast redwoods have the record for height. But there is another type of redwood that has a much bigger trunk. In 1852, in the Sierra Nevada Mountains of central California, a man named A.T. Dowd went hunting. He shot and wounded a grizzly bear. The bear fled deep into the forest. Dowd followed the wounded beast. Suddenly he came to a enormous wall of red wood. He looked up. It wasn't a wall, it was a tree! But this tree was bigger than any tree he had ever seen before. The trunk was forty feet across, and it seemed to rise up to the clouds. Dowd ran back to camp to tell his friends.

Giant sequoias have bigger trunks than coast redwoods.

WHAT DO GIANT SEQUOIAS LOOK LIKE?

The trees discovered by A.T. Dowd are called *giant sequoias* (suh-KWOY-uh). They live only in the Sierra Nevada Mountains. Sequoias are related to the coast redwoods, but they have thicker trunks. Their needles are also shorter, and their cones are larger—about the size of an apricot. Sequoias also live much longer. You can tell the age of a tree by counting the number of rings in its trunk. The oldest sequoias are over 3,500 years old!

Giant sequoias have a thick trunk.

WHAT'S THE BIGGEST REDWOOD OF ALL?

Some of the largest sequoias have been given names. The biggest of them all is the General Sherman tree. Imagine a tree with a trunk as big around as your classroom! If you have thirty kids in your class, and you all hold hands and make a big circle, that's how big around it is. The General Sherman is 272 feet tall. It weighs 12,000,000 pounds, and it is more than 100 feet around. The lowest branch of the General Sherman starts 130 feet above the ground. The branch is 7 feet across and 125 feet long. That one branch is bigger than most trees! The General Sherman tree is the largest living thing on our planet.

The General Sherman tree is the largest sequoia tree.

IS THERE A THIRD TYPE OF REDWOOD?

In 1944, a Chinese **forester** found a grove of unusual-looking trees in a **remote** area of central China. The trees had needles like pine trees, and thick reddish bark. And they stood 150 feet tall! Scientists soon realized that they had discovered a third type of redwood.

The new tree was called the *dawn redwood*. It has been found only in two tiny areas of central China. Dawn redwoods are now protected by the Chinese government.

Dawn redwoods have needles like pine trees.

HOW CAN REDWOODS LIVE SO LONG?

Redwood trees are built to last. Their wide, shallow roots grip the earth, helping them stand up to the worst storms. They can live through long dry spells and terrible floods. Even a forest fire can't hurt a big redwood. The outer layer of redwood bark burns easily, but the second layer of bark is thick and moist. The flame sputters and goes out before the tree is hurt. Redwoods are tough trees!

But there is one thing that can kill a redwood in minutes. A man with a chain saw!

Redwood bark can stand up to fire.

ARE REDWOODS IN DANGER?

In the late 1800s, the coast redwood forests were nearly destroyed by **logging**. The soft, red-colored wood lasts a long time and holds up in all kinds of weather. Redwood does not rot like other kinds of wood. A picnic table made from redwood will last for many years.

San Francisco was built out of redwood. The redwood forests near the city were all chopped down. Soon, the city of San Francisco was surrounded by bare, treeless hills.

Redwood trees were cut down for their soft, red-colored wood.

ARE GIANT SEQUOIAS IN DANGER?

The giant sequoias were also logged. It took a group of strong **lumberjacks** two or three days to cut down one large sequoia. Some of the biggest and oldest trees were chopped down, cut into pieces, and shipped to cities. There, they were put on display for the public. Other trees were cut down and made into fence posts and patio furniture.

People were angry that these great trees were being destroyed. A **naturalist** named John Muir wrote books and articles about what was happening to the sequoias.

Giant sequoias were cut down by loggers.

HOW ARE REDWOODS PROTECTED?

In 1890, John Muir convinced the government to form national parks to protect the sequoias. Over the next fifty years, the government slowly bought the sequoia forests and made them national parks. Today, nearly all of the sequoias are located in our national parks and forests. Giant sequoias are no longer cut down for displays or made into patio furniture.

Most sequoias are located in national parks.

The giant sequoias were saved, but the coast redwood forests were still being destroyed. Finally, in 1968, Congress established Redwood National Park. This park protected 30,000 acres of redwood forests. Ten years later, the park was expanded to 78,000 acres.

Coast redwoods are still cut down for lumber, but the cutting is now controlled. Trees that are cut down are replaced by new trees. The largest and oldest coast redwoods will never be cut down—they are protected by the U.S. government.

Redwood National Park was created to protect redwoods.

Redwood trees are a national treasure. Their age takes us back to a time long before Europeans set foot in America. Their awesome size shows us the power and wonder of nature. But nature is also fragile. Even the mighty redwoods need our protection.

One day you might visit a grove of giant sequoias. Maybe next year. Or the year after that. Or in fifty years. You can take your time, because they will still be there, standing tall, reaching for the clouds.

Redwood trees reach for the clouds.

GLOSSARY

forester (fore-ES-ter)
A person who is trained to work in the forest. A forestor discovered the dawn redwood.

remote (re-MOAT)
A location that is away from largely populated areas. Dawn redwoods are found in a remote area of China.

logging (LOG-eng)
The act of cutting down trees. Coast redwood trees were nearly destroyed by logging.

lumberjacks (LUM-burr-jax)
One engaged in logging. It takes a group of lumberjacks two or three days to cut down a large sequoia.

naturalist (NAT-er-all-ist)
One that believes in studying the natural world. A naturalist named John Muir wrote books and articles about the sequoias.

INDEX